breakfast breads . . . gift loaves . . . nutritious whole grains . . . fruit-and-nut breads . . . fat-free Lemon Poppy Seed Bread . . . Peanut Butter Chocolate Chip Bread . . . Spinach Feta Cheese Bread . . . Mozzarella Cheese and Sun-Dried Tomato Bread

DO YOU KNOW . . .

- ◆ How to determine which bread machine is the right one for you?
- ◆ Why a yeast dispenser is one of the best features to look for?
- ◆ What adding milk will do for a bread's flavor and longevity?
- ◆ Why you should store bread in paper, not plastic?
- ◆ Which yeast will give the best results?
- ◆ How much to spend for a bread knife . . . and why?
- ◆ How to substitute applesauce for sugar in bread recipes?
- ◆ Which brand-name prepackaged mixes consistently produce wonderful, well-risen loaves . . . and which don't?
- ◆ How you can wake up to the smell of freshly baked bread . . . or have a ready-to-eat loaf waiting when you get home from work?

FRESH HOMEMADE BREAD IS ONE
OF LIFE'S SPECIAL PLEASURES.
ENJOY IT WITH . . .

WHAT CAN I DO WITH
MY BREAD MACHINE?

Also by Barbara Norman

WHAT CAN I DO WITH MY JUICER?

WHAT CAN I DO WITH MY BREAD MACHINE?

Barbara Norman

A DELL BOOK

Published by
Dell Publishing
a division of
Bantam Doubleday Dell Publishing Group, Inc.
1540 Broadway
New York, New York 10036

ISBN: 0-440-22048-3

DESIGN: Stanley S. Drate/Folio Graphics Co., Inc.

Printed in the United States of America

Published simultaneously in Canada

July 1995

10 9 8 7 6 5 4 3 2 1

OPM

To Viola and Gabriel
Cohn, wonderfully
unique parents

CONTENTS

---◆---

WHAT
CAN I DO
WITH MY
BREAD
MACHINE?

INTRODUCTION

---◆---

What Can I Do with My Bread Machine?

B Breads, bagels, and brioches can be freshly baked with a minimal amount of effort.

R Rising of the dough, which used to take an uncertain amount of time, becomes automatic with your bread machine; with a window in your machine, you can even watch.

E Exotic creations as well as good old-fashioned basic breads are quick and easy to make.

A A + + + is the grade you will receive for treats made with your bread machine.

D Dough that is made with little more effort than measuring ingredients and pressing a button provides the basis for shaped breads, rolls, coffee cakes, sweet rolls, or breadsticks.

M Mixes are specially made for bread machines and contribute an array of options and flavors *if all you want to do is add water.*

A All varieties of soft pretzels, including sesame, poppy seed, salt, onion, and herb, are ready whenever you crave them.

C Croutons, made to order, are yours by slicing day-old bread, sprinkling with olive oil or butter, adding herbs or spices, and baking.

H Herbs and spices, fresh, homegrown, or dried, provide an endless variety of flavors for hours of delicious experimentation.

I Ingredients you need to produce all these fabulous treats are those normally found in your pantry.

N Nutritional and dietary needs—from less salt to no added fat—are easily implemented with your bread machine.

E ENJOY . . . and read on!

I

◆

It's Simple and Quick to Make Delicious Bread

Few kitchen aromas are as easily identifiable as freshly baked bread. Whether you awaken to its fragrance in anticipation of a continental or full breakfast, arrive home just before the bread is ready for a main course of soup, or anticipate BLTs with homemade toast, freshly baked bread makes each meal a special one.

Until recently the pleasure of freshly baked warm bread was reserved for those adventurous cooks who were willing to put in the time and effort (not to mention the mess at home). With the advent of bread machines, warm, freshly baked bread of all varieties can be enjoyed regularly and with a minimum of effort. But that's not all. Your bread machine also makes delicious bagels, pizza, pretzels, focaccia, rolls, rice, and even jam.

1

The simplicity of the bread machine is truly astonishing. Friends, without exception, inquire, "Is it really that simple to bake bread with the machine?" and add, "Does the bread taste as good as the real thing?" The answer to each question is a resounding "Yes!" and it gets even better! With the simplicity of the bread machine you can carefully control both the flavors and the ingredients in your bread and other treats. This means eliminating salt, fats, eggs, and spices to accommodate special tastes and dietary needs. It also means combining favorite ingredients and flavors to achieve perfect results for personal preferences.

II

◆

Bread Machine Basics

1. *How Your Bread Machine Works*

If you've ever baked a loaf of bread or know the steps involved, the simplicity with which the bread machine turns out consistently outstanding loaves sounds *almost* too good to be true. Yet it is true that freshly baked bread can be yours with a few simple steps that include: (1) pouring the dry, then the wet ingredients into the machine (depending on your machine, you may need to add the wet, then the dry); next, (2) adding yeast either directly or through the separate yeast dispenser; and finally, (3) pressing the start button. Your loaf will be finished in from three to thirteen hours depending on whether you use the timer. All machines include a variety of cycles, such as mix, rest, knead, and rise,

3

to produce a finished loaf. When the machine's beep alerts you that the bread is ready, open the door, and *with a potholder* pull out the bread pan, turn it upside down to release the loaf, and place it on a rack to cool. Cleaning the bread pan is a breeze: You merely wipe it with a soft cloth or gently rinse it with mild soap and warm water. THAT IS IT!

You may select a machine with more options, including quick rise, whole wheat functions, dough preparation only, quick bread, rice, or even jam maker. Using the dough cycle along with a little work, you can make pizza, focaccia, pretzels, bagels, and rolls.

2. *Selecting a Bread Machine Right for You*

Selecting a bread machine is a simple process if you have a little bit of information going in. You are the only one who can decide which options and size machine are right for you. There are a number of options and manufacturers (currently there are at least fourteen manufacturers offering one or two models each) with the number increasing every season. Each store you visit will most likely carry a selection of one to five machines.

Mail-order catalogs and television shopping clubs also are offering several models. Whether you purchase your machine in person at a store, or from a mail-order company or the television, there are several factors to consider. They are listed here in order of importance based on my personal experience and preference.

SIZE OF LOAF

How much can you eat? Depending on how many people are in your family and how many are serious bread eaters, you should first determine whether you need a one- or one-and-one-half-pound loaf machine. One-pound loaves from bread machines are either square or round (approximately 5″ × 5″ × 7″) and produce eight to ten slices. One-and-one-half-pound loaves from bread machines are either the traditional horizontally shaped rectangular loaves (approximately 7″ × 4½″ × 7″) or the same size around as the one-pound loaf, only taller, resulting in a vertically shaped rectangular loaf (5″ × 5″ × 8″) that produces ten to fourteen thick slices. (Panasonic even informs me that its "one-pound" machine actually makes a one-and-one-quarter-pound loaf and that its "one-and-one-half-pound" machine makes a one-and-three-quarter-pound loaf.)

There is even a two-pound loaf machine. Although the number of two-pound machines on the market is growing, at the present time most available machines as well as recipes are for one- or one-and-one-half-pound breads. Because it is so easy to make additional loaves, a one- or one-and-one-half-pound loaf is sufficient for a small family for a one-to two-day period. A two-pound loaf would be preferred primarily for a party or large family. But even for a party, I would suggest creating two smaller loaves so you can serve either a variety of breads or perhaps serve both bread and rolls or breadsticks.

For purposes of this chapter, the one- and one-and-one-half-pound machines are considered. If you opt for a two-pound machine, you need to consider these features as well.

SIZE AND WEIGHT OF MACHINE

Because counter space is at such a premium with all the useful machines you want to include in your kitchen, you need to determine how much space you have to allocate to your bread machine. Even machines making identical size loaves of bread vary in size. For example, one-pound loaf machines I have used range from $12'' \times 10'' \times 12''$ to $10'' \times 14'' \times 14''$. Machines also vary in weight from fourteen to twenty pounds.

SEPARATE YEAST DISPENSER

Adding the yeast through a separate compartment in the top of the machine rather than with the rest of the dry ingredients is an option available from some manufacturers. It is my experience that having a separate yeast dispenser contributes to foolproof breadmaking especially if you are going to be using the timer feature regularly (see below). When using your machine's delayed timer without a separate yeast dispenser, you must take great care to ensure that you do not touch the dry yeast to the wet ingredients. If you do, the yeast process will begin too soon, and the result will be a less than perfect loaf. With a dispenser, the dry yeast is added through the separate compartment at the top of the machine at precisely the right time (when you use the timer feature, this is most likely to occur while you are fast asleep!) The yeast drops and meets the wet ingredients at just the moment necessary to ensure the greatest rising success.

TIMER

This feature is great if you dream of awakening to the luscious smell of home-baked bread. Who doesn't? Or if you want to have a loaf waiting for you when you arrive home from work just before dinner. Or you may even set the timer during the day so the loaf will be baking as you get ready for a dinner party so you do not even have to think about making the bread while you are preparing the meal. By presetting your machine anywhere from three to thirteen hours (some machines can be set as far as twenty-four hours in advance of ETA), you can time with precision when the loaf will be finished.

VARIETY OF CYCLES

All bread machines bake bread. Most also include a cycle to produce unbaked dough, which you can use to shape your own breads, breadsticks, or rolls that you then bake in your traditional oven. Many machines add rapid bake cycles, which accomplish faster production time either by including only one rising instead of two or by shortening the total rising time. Some have a feature that allows you to determine how crispy or how dark your crust is. Since I have never produced a loaf that wasn't fabulously crispy, this feature does not seem an important one to me.

Machines that make consistently very crispy loaves are the Panasonic and Zojirushi. Machines may include whole wheat or multigrain cycles, which allow the blade to mix and bake this heavier dough without faltering. They also have longer rising times. Even though bread made with all whole wheat flour has a very heavy texture that not all bakers will choose, the whole wheat feature on your machine is extremely useful for baking and experimenting with many types of grains and flours. Using a variety of grains and flours may make breads heavier than those made with all bread flour, and the whole wheat feature will accommodate these variety loaves. By allowing for a more thorough mixing of the ingredients and a longer rising time, this feature will make tastier, better-textured loaves.

8

PRICE VARIANCES

With so many models and with competition increasing monthly, prices have come down from their original highs of three hundred dollars or more. Currently you can find in the two-hundred-dollar range excellent bread machines that produce consistently delicious loaves. Still, prices range from about one hundred to four hundred dollars. The machines producing larger loaves cost slightly more; the "no-name" and "little-known" brands cost less. One was advertised recently at a discount store for fifty-nine dollars!

CLEANING CONCERNS

All the machines on the market have separate bread pans with handles that may be taken out of the machines. Because the heating elements and heating sensors are on the inside of the machines, care must be taken in cleaning them. The Zojirushi comes with a removable pan for the machine floor to catch the loose crumbs. I have found that cleanup is much easier when you can lift out the crumb catcher and wash it separately. On the other machines, to remove crumbs from the bottom, you must turn the machines upside down or place a vacuum cleaner head inside (look in Chapter IX, "Hints and Suggestions"). Portable vacuums as well as attachments to your full-size vacuum can be used. The cleaning of all machines is similar although some are easier to get your hand into to wipe the inside. On some machines the top lid can be removed, supposedly for easier cleaning. This is reminiscent of the feature that lets you remove the oven door completely for easier cleaning. Do *you* do it? Neither do I!

COOLING CYCLE

Some bread machines have a cooling cycle that circulates air around a finished baked loaf. If you are not available to remove the loaf immediately when it is done and you are concerned that the moisture built up in the machine may make the crust limp or soggy, you might look into this option. Consider your need for this option carefully, because it could add up to one hundred dollars to the price of your machine.

QUICK BREAD CYCLE

While you bought your machine to make bread, an option to consider is the quick bread cycle, which turns out wonderful yeastless, moist cakes, zucchini breads, and even cakes from cake mixes. One of the machines in which this helpful option works extremely well is the Zojirushi. The largest Panasonic model also has a quick bread cycle. The cake it produces is in the shape of a square loaf of bread, but the taste is the same as it would be if baked in a traditional oven. I recently made a cake from a chocolate cake mix on the quick bread cycle, and it drew rave reviews.

Now the options get even more interesting.

VIEWING WINDOW

If you like to watch while the bread is rising and baking, consider a machine with a window. Some windows, such as that in the Hitachi model I own, are very small and difficult to see through. Others permit you to watch your bread progress through each stage. A viewing window also lets you see if the bread is mixing properly. During my second time using a new Zojirushi machine with a larger window, I looked through the window and saw that the dough was not mixing. I stopped the machine, pulled out the bread pan, and saw that the blade was not properly installed in place. I made the correction, placed the ingredients back in the pan, and the process continued without a hitch. Had it not been for the window, I would have waited for three to four hours, pulled out the bread pan, and had a concoction that was not bread, but rather an incredible heap of unmixed and baked ingredients. (Among other things this experience has taught me to make sure that the mixing blade is placed firmly on its post when I use any machine.)

RICE MAKER

Ever thought of making rice with your "bread machine"? Some Hitachi models have incorporated a rice maker feature to convert your bread machine to a rice maker. Although at first the idea took some getting used to, this feature made more sense to me when I saw it as an option to buying a separate rice steamer. I have made rice several times, and the texture was consistently excellent. The fifty-five minutes it takes to make the rice is somewhat longer than making it conventionally on the stove. When considering whether or not to purchase a machine with the rice option, determine if you are going to buy a separate rice steamer. If you have no plans to purchase a separate rice steamer anyway, forget it.

JAM MAKER

You've got to be kidding. Make jam in a bread machine? How is this possible? This feature really surprised me too. Is it just an unnecessary option to add to the price of the machine and make you feel as if you are getting something special? After all, do you ever use *all* the options on your multioption dishwasher or washing machine? Neither do I! Out of curiosity, though, I tried making strawberry jam in the machine, and was it great! With the jam maker the stove did not have to be turned on, and the time needed to make the jam was measured with precision. The quantity was small (one cup), but the flavor was delicious. I have made jam in both the Hitachi and the Zojirushi machines and have not been disappointed by either. The only ingredients needed to make jam are fruit (my preference is for strawberries), sugar, water, and lemon juice. The fresh flavor of bread machine jam is suitable for not only bread and toast but also topping on ice cream and cake. One word of caution: After the jam is made, be sure to rinse and clean the bread pan thoroughly and promptly. Failure to do so could result in damage to your bread pan's nonstick finish.

All the machines tested bake good loaves of bread, with some producing great and crispy loaves consistently. With so many machines on the market I have not used all of them, and so I cannot attempt to give a comprehensive brand rating. Instead I am commenting on distinctive features or concerns I had with the individual machines I have used.

3. Equipment and Supplies You Will Need

There are hundreds of gadgets and gizmos you can buy to make bread, but there are only a few you must have. These are listed below in order of importance.

POTHOLDERS

There is one warning which all potential bread-makers must heed: ALWAYS USE POTHOLDERS WHEN REMOVING BREAD FROM THE MACHINE AND WHEN REMOVING THE BREAD FROM THE PAN. Your enthusiasm for a just-finished loaf will come to a sudden halt if a hot pan is touched without a pot-holder. Do not make this mistake.

MEASURING CUPS

Because the success of your loaves may be closely tied to properly measured ingredients, it is essential to have a standard set of measuring cups, for both liquid and dry ingredients. Just estimating certain ingredients when making bread will not do! Using one-half cup of wheat flour when you are supposed to use only one-quarter could make the difference between bread turning out like a doorstop or a delicious, dense, crumbly textured delight. A set of measuring cups for dry ingredients should include one, one-half, one-third, and one-quarter cup sizes. The liquid ingredients should be measured in a one- to four-cup glass/clear measuring cup. Most machines come with a measuring cup and spoons, some even indicating right on them the ingredient they are to be used to measure: water, salt, yeast, dry milk, sugar, etc. Frankly I haven't found these utensils useful. They can get lost in the back of drawers and cupboards. Furthermore, if you are improvising or experimenting with the amounts called for in the recipe, using these cups and spoons, which have only the names of the ingredients to be measured without the amounts on them, can be very frustrating

MEASURING SPOONS

A standard set of measuring spoons includes one tablespoon, one-half tablespoon, one teaspoon, one-half teaspoon, and one-quarter teaspoon. When a recipe calls for only a fraction of a spoon of ingredients, do not estimate these small portions with regular soup or coffee spoons from your silverware drawer. Using one teaspoon of dry yeast or a heaping coffee spoon full can mean the difference between a beautifully risen loaf and one that goes out of control and hits the top of the bread machine while baking. This is not to say that all ingredients must be perfectly measured. There are exceptions. Adding one or two tablespoons of poppy seeds to the Lemon Poppy Seed Bread (page 80) is solely dependent on personal preference. Whether you add one or two teaspoons of vanilla to the Honey Apricot Walnut Loaf (page 74) will be noticed only by the most discriminating of palates. In Chapter IX ("Hints and Suggestions," page 119), you will see that in many recipes cutting the fat from one tablespoon of butter to one-third tablespoon of butter or eliminating it altogether makes little difference in the taste of the bread. With herbs, liquids, dried fruits and nuts, you can also get creative.

COOLING RACKS

When your bread comes out of the oven, it is essential that it cool on a rack. A plain wire cake cooling rack works perfectly.

BREAD KNIVES

The most expensive bread knives are not necessarily the best for cutting bread. After hearing from all my cooking teachers and reading in all the cooking magazines to buy only the best (usually implying the most expensive) bread knives, I conducted my own test. I made three breads from identical ingredients and put three knives of various cost and quality to the test. The knives included the kitchen knife that has been in our kitchen for more than twenty-five years, with no name, probably from a collection of knives received as a wedding gift; a bread knife of the stainless steel variety, moderately priced (six-dollar range) and claiming it "never has to be sharpened"; and the primo knife in the sixty-five-dollar category, claiming to be the ultimate in kitchen cutlery. While it's true that the moderately priced bread knife and the expensive variety cut the breads more easily and with less crushing than the old knife from my wedding set, the difference between the moderately priced and the expensive knives was insignificant. I suppose their durability and endurance will be tested months and years down the road when they begin to dull and sharpening is necessary, but for now it's safe to say that a moderately priced bread knife is just fine.

PLASTIC BAGS

Be sure to have several sizes of these kitchen necessities on hand for breadmaking, including one-half-gallon and one-gallon bags. Depending on what size loaves you bake, the one-half-gallon and one-gallon sizes can be used to make your own prepackaged bread mixes (see Chapter IV, "Prepackaged Mixes [or Simplifying Bread Making]"). Both sizes can be used to store bread, but be sure to wait until a bread has completely cooled before putting it into a plastic bag. If you place a warm bread in a plastic bag, it will develop a soggy crust very quickly. Smaller plastic bags can be used to store leftover ingredients for use at a later time.

PAPER BAGS

Keep plain paper bags from the grocery to store freshly baked bread. They prevent warm breads from developing soggy crusts although the breads will dry out if not eaten fairly rapidly. This should

not be a problem because freshly baked bread dis-
appears so quickly, and it is unlikely you will not
finish a loaf in a day's time.

BAKING SHEETS AND PANS

For rolls, breadsticks, sweet rolls, pretzels, focaccia, or bagels you need two baking or cookie
sheets. If you will be making round coffee cakes or
pizzas, you need eight- or nine-inch round cake
pans.

It's not actually necessary but it is fun to have
these supplies:

DECORATIVE PAPER BAGS AND TISSUE
PAPER

How pretty to wrap a loaf in festive tissues or
bags! Because bread is such a treat, giving a loaf
to a friend is always appreciated. For presenting
the loaf, have plain white bags on hand or for a
couple of extra dollars, order personalized bags
from a mail-order novelty company. "From the
Kitchen of [Your Name]" and "Bread from [Your
Name]" are two popular phrases available. You may
wrap the bread loosely in colorful or decorated tis-
sue paper before placing it in the bag. A bow or
ribbon adds even more festivity and fun to the gift.

A VARIETY OF CUTTING BOARDS, CRUMB CATCHERS, PIZZA CUTTERS, AND PASTRY BRUSHES

These items can be fun and helpful additions, but obviously are not mandatory to making great bread and treats.

4. Ingredients to Have on Hand

There is no reason why you have to purchase special ingredients to make fabulous bread every time. For new types of bread, you can experiment with new spices or types of flour, but you can also make sensational bread with absolutely no unusual ingredients or extra trips to the grocery. The one exception is the purchase of bread flour, which most people do not have in their pantries at home.

FLOURS

Forget what you've heard or have been led to believe in your general cookbooks, bread cookbooks, magazine articles, and cooking classes. The truth is there are only three types of flour that you need to make fabulous bread. They are bread, all-purpose, and whole wheat flour. All others may be required for special recipes or dietary requirements but are *not* de rigueur in your kitchen bread pantry. Breads made with bread flour will be lighter in texture than those made with one or more whole grains. The baking section of your grocery may include other flours, most commonly rye and pumpernickel. There are also a multitude of types of flours from specialty groceries, health food stores, bakery supply stores, and mail-order companies. If they are suitable to be used in bread recipes, they generally require specific instructions. Use them only if you wish, and be sure to check recipes for special instructions if you use such flours as buckwheat, millet, oat, rice, potato, soy, spelt, and others.

The Big Three

1. Bread flour: This is a "strong" flour with a high-protein, high gluten-producing content. Gluten causes bread to rise better and creates an elastic texture. Purists may claim that adding gluten to cake flour is a more authentic way of baking, but why go through that unnecessary step? Buy the bread flour and adding gluten is not necessary.

2. All-purpose flour: Don't panic if you use all-purpose flour instead of bread flour when you are making bread. All-purpose flour is what we were raised on to bake cakes and cookies and to add to gravies. It is a "weaker" flour than bread, having a lower protein content. Because it does not have a high gluten content, you may generally not use it as the only flour in bread recipes. Some recipes call for partial all-purpose flour combined with wheat or rye flour. Do not substitute all-purpose flour for

bread flour. The results will not be disastrous, as one new owner of a bread machine found out, but the bread with all-purpose flour does not rise as well, nor does it have the rich yeast flavor or chewy texture of bread made with bread flour.

3. Whole wheat flour: To make a wheat or whole grain bread, some or all of the flour is whole wheat. Whole wheat flour is made by grinding the entire wheat kernel. Some bread machines accommodate a bread made from a large percentage of whole wheat flour, yet this bread has a texture that is extremely dense. (One loaf I made could have doubled for a doorstop and tripled for a shot put!) For a whole wheat loaf with a softer texture use partial (one-quarter to one-half) whole wheat flour, with the remainder all-purpose or bread flour.

—The Other Players

Rye and Pumpernickel Flours

Although not among the Big Three, these flours may be used in small amounts along with some of the Big Three to make breads varying in texture and flavor.

Cake Flour

Cake flour is a very low protein content flour that *will not make good bread when used by itself.* When a recipe calls for cake flour in the bread machine, it is always added to another type of flour.

DO NOT USE SELF-RISING FLOUR.

FAT

It takes little or no fat to make fine loaves of bread. Most bread recipes include fat as an ingredient. Why? Fats add richness, flavor, moisture, and tenderness to the texture of bread. A delicate crust is often the result of only one tablespoon of butter in a recipe. Most one-pound bread recipes in this book use one tablespoon of butter or fat. Sweet butter is recommended. Unsalted margarine or a butter/margarine blend may be substituted for unsalted butter. With the exception of Special Coffee Cake Bread with Dried Fruit (page 61), no recipe in this book calls for more than two tablespoons of butter or oil for a one-pound loaf and three for a one-and-one-half-pound loaf.

Oils are the fat recommended in some recipes. For a fabulous Spinach Feta Cheese Bread (page 96) only olive oil will do. Although many general recipes call for either vegetable or olive oil, for pizza and focaccia I prefer olive oil. Where no specific oil is listed, all-purpose vegetable, canola, safflower, or corn oil is recommended. You will begin to create your own personal repertoire of ingredients as you experiment.

THE EFFECT OF REDUCING FAT IN RECIPES: In most recipes in which the fat was reduced to as little as one-quarter of the amount specified in recipes (from one tablespoon to one-quarter tablespoon), the crust was a bit tougher and the flavor was only slightly affected. The bread was still better than store-bought.

YEAST

Yeast is an essential ingredient in making breads that have the chewy, pull-apart texture we associate with homemade bread. Some breads, such as quick breads and beer breads, that do not use yeast have a completely different texture and flavor from the breads that use it. Yeast is the ingredient that makes bread rise and accounts for the chemical process of the inclusion of air and lightness in dough and bread.

Yeast comes in two basic types: dry granulated and fresh. In the dry granulated variety there is the regular fast-acting yeast and, most recently in stores, a bread machine yeast. Bread machine yeast is more finely granulated than regular dry and disperses more thoroughly during mixing and kneading. Some yeast distributors and bread machine manufacturers recommend a quick-rising dry yeast for bread, while others recommend a regular-acting dry yeast. Consult your manufacturer's directions to determine if either type is recommended for your machine. Once you determine which type of dry yeast you will use, you may buy it in one-quarter-ounce packets or small jars in the refrigerator section of your grocery.

At a food club I recently purchased an institutional size (one pound) of dry yeast in a sealed bag. Although yeast has a usage date stamped on it and, once opened, may stay fresh in your refrigerator for three months, you would want to buy yeast in smaller sizes to ensure freshness. Few things are as frustrating in breadmaking as to measure carefully all the ingredients, patiently wait for the finished loaf, only to find that the yeast is not fresh and consequently the bread does not rise properly. Watch dates carefully, and try to buy only the amount of yeast you can comfortably use in a two-month period.

Just as exasperating as using old yeast is completely forgetting to add the yeast. Because the yeast is the last ingredient added to the recipe, the prepackaged mix, or the separate yeast dispenser, it is easy to overlook this essential ingredient.

SALT

An entire loaf of bread does not have to include more than one-quarter to one teaspoon of salt, or it may even be eliminated completely in some breads. Salt is the ingredient that strengthens the gluten structure, makes the dough elastic, and adds flavor. It also prevents the yeast from overrising.

The inclusion of salt in bread recipes is standard, yet varying the amounts of salt used has had little effect on the results of the recipes in this book.

THE EFFECT OF REDUCING SALT IN RECIPES: Especially when watching salt intake for dietary or health reasons, you will have great pleasure in knowing that lowering the salt in most recipes from one teaspoon to one-quarter makes little difference in the finished product. Salt does act to slow down the action of the yeast. Numerous tests showed that the taste and rising of the breads varied little with the adjustment of the salt from one to one-quarter teaspoon. Still, if you do not have specific dietary or health requirements or commitments, use the amount of salt specified in the recipes.

A coarser salt, sold as kosher salt, makes a preferred topping for bagels, pretzels, and rolls. It is sold in most supermarkets. Do not substitute kosher salt for regular salt in recipes.

MILK

Milk adds flavor and contributes to a richer, softer, golden crust. Whole or nonfat dry milk is used in the recipes in this book. When you use nonfat dry milk, it is necessary to add water or liquid to reconstitute the milk in the recipe. If a recipe calls for one cup of whole milk and you have only nonfat dry milk, simply substitute enough dry milk and water to equal the amount of whole milk specified. Skim milk may be substituted for whole or nonfat dry milk.

SUGAR AND SWEETENERS

Sugar or alternative sweeteners stimulate the action of the yeast and keep the bread soft. They also add flavor and color. Too much sugar may decrease the action of the yeast; too little affects taste. When a recipe calls for sugar, an equal amount of brown sugar may be substituted. To substitute honey, maple syrup, or molasses, decrease the amount of liquid by the same amount of wet sweetener used. For example, when a recipe calls for one tablespoon of sugar and one cup of water, you may substitute one tablespoon of honey if you decrease the water by one tablespoon so that you have one cup minus one tablespoon of water ($^{15}\!/_{16}$ cup). You can also eliminate sugar by substituting unsweetened applesauce for all or part of the water in the recipe. Applesauce-sweetened bread is especially appealing for peanut butter sandwiches.

NUTS

Walnuts, pecans, macadamia nuts, peanuts, or almonds add great texture and taste to many of your favorite breads and rolls. Nuts may be toasted or roasted or used raw, and they should be chopped into one-quarter-inch pieces before being added to dry ingredients. Even if nuts are added after the first kneading, they still may be pulverized by the mixing blade of the bread machine. Consult your manufacturer's instructions for the best point at which to add nuts to the dough.

FRUIT

An ordinary loaf turns into a sweet snack or dessert bread with the addition of pieces of such fruits as apricots, dates, cherries, apples, cranberries, and prunes. Fresh, dried, frozen, or canned, fruits provide endless new combinations for breads. When improvising and using frozen or canned fruit, be sure to adjust the liquid content of the recipe. (See Chapter V, "A–Z Recipes and Ideas," page 47.)

EGGS

Eggs added to a recipe soften the bread and give it more color and richness. Because eggs are high in cholesterol, you may substitute egg whites (do so by the total measurement of the liquid, not by the number of eggs) or egg substitutes. One-quarter cup of egg substitute can be used to replace each egg. Do not use eggs or egg substitutes if you are using the timer feature on your machine, because of the potential for spoilage.

SPICES AND HERBS

Fresh or dried spices and herbs from your garden or your pantry add interesting flavors to familiar recipes. Herbs, such as basil, thyme, rosemary, dill, and parsley, left in pieces make attractive and tasty toppings for focaccia, pizza, and rolls. When dry herbs and spices are used, less is needed. For example, two tablespoons of chopped fresh dill are the equivalent of one tablespoon of dry. Add the spices or herbs to the dry ingredients.

You may use any spices you buy or grow in your garden, fresh or dry: lemon basil or verbena added to a lemon loaf; oregano, dill, parsley, chives, or thyme to an herb loaf; cinnamon, vanilla, or orange or lemon peel to a citrus loaf. The list could go on and on. Use your imagination.

III

◆

Basic Bread Recipes

YOU CANNOT GO WRONG IF YOU USE THE FOL-
LOWING RECIPES TO FAMILIARIZE YOURSELF WITH
YOUR BREAD MACHINE AND TO BECOME COMFORT-
ABLE EXPERIMENTING.

Although all machines differ, certain bread recipes seem to work well in most machines. Here are
basic recipes for making both one- and one-half-
pound loaves of bread. Also try the recommended
basic recipes that come with your machine. When
you determine which you like best, use these recipes to prepare your own prepackaged mixes as well
as to personalize bread specialties with your favorite additions.

A Note About Making Your First Loaf

Making your first loaf should be fun. Don't panic.
It is easier than you think.

All bread machine manufacturers include recipes, pamphlets, and even videotapes with their machines. Each manufacturer suggests several basic recipes that work especially well in its machine. Although the recipes for most machines are similar, they may vary slightly in the amounts of basic ingredients, especially the liquids and yeast. The first few times you make bread, you will get to know your machine. Each one has variations in the lengths of cycles, the noises it makes, and how much leeway you have in varying the ingredients called for in the recipes.

I suggest that your first loaf be one of the basic recipes for white, wheat, or egg bread included with your machine. If you are especially timid about making your first loaves, you may even want to use prepackaged mixes before you try your manufacturer's suggested recipes for basic loaves. That way you can learn about your machine while determining which breads you prefer. The recipes included by the manufacturer may become the basis of what will be in your breadmaking repertoire. Once you determine your machine's best basic recipes or find a prepackaged basic mix you like, a potpourri of breads will be yours when you know what spices, nuts, fruits, or ingredients can be added to create variety and interesting tasty alternatives to plain white or wheat bread.

Basic White Bread

◆

RECIPE FOR A ONE-POUND LOAF

*2¼ cups bread flour
*1 tablespoon dry milk
*1 teaspoon salt
*1½ tablespoons sugar
⅞ cup water
1 tablespoon butter or margarine
1¼ teaspoons dry yeast

If you are using this recipe to prepackage a mix of your own, pack the dry ingredients listed with an * and do not add the remaining ingredients until you are ready to bake the bread.

RECIPE FOR A ONE-AND-ONE-HALF-POUND LOAF

*3⅛ cups bread flour
*1½ tablespoons dry milk
*1½ teaspoons salt
*2 tablespoons sugar
1¼ cups water
1½ tablespoons butter
2 teaspoons dry yeast

If you are using this recipe to prepackage a mix of your own, pack the dry ingredients listed with an * and do not add the remaining ingredients until you are ready to bake the bread.

31

DIRECTIONS: Place all the ingredients in the bread pan in the order recommended by the manufacturer. Program the machine for the white bread cycle, and bake the bread. When it has finished baking, remove the pan from the machine with potholders or oven mitts. Turn the bread pan upside down, and shake the loaf out of the pan. Place the bread on a wire rack to cool.

Basic Wheat Combo Bread

RECIPE FOR A ONE-POUND LOAF

> *1¼ cups wheat flour
> *1 cup bread flour
> *1 tablespoon dry milk
> *1 teaspoon salt
> *1 tablespoon sugar
> ⅞ cup water
> 1 tablespoon butter or margarine
> 1½ teaspoons dry yeast

If you are using this recipe to prepackage a mix of your own, pack the dry ingredients listed with an * and do not add the remaining ingredients until you are ready to bake the bread.

RECIPE FOR A ONE-AND-ONE-HALF-POUND LOAF

> *1¾ cups wheat flour
> *1½ cups bread flour
> *1½ tablespoons dry milk
> *1½ teaspoons salt
> *1½ tablespoons sugar
> 1⅛ cups water
> 1½ tablespoons butter or margarine
> 2 teaspoons dry yeast

If you are using this recipe to prepackage a mix of your own, pack the dry ingredients listed with an * and do not add the remaining ingredients until you are ready to bake the bread.

DIRECTIONS: Place all the ingredients in the bread pan in the order recommended by the manufacturer. Program the machine for the wheat bread cycle, and bake the bread. When it has finished baking, remove the pan from the machine with potholders or oven mitts. Turn the bread pan upside down, and shake the loaf out of the pan. Place the bread on a wire rack to cool.

33

Egg Bread (Do not use the automatic timer feature with this bread)

◆

RECIPE FOR A ONE-POUND LOAF

> *2¼ cups bread flour
> *1 tablespoon dry milk
> *¾ teaspoon salt
> *1 tablespoon sugar
> ¾ cup water
> 1 egg
> 1 tablespoon butter or margarine
> 1½ teaspoons dry yeast

If you are using this recipe to prepackage a mix of your own, pack the dry ingredients listed with an * and do not add remaining ingredients until you are ready to bake the bread.

RECIPE FOR A ONE-AND-ONE-HALF-POUND LOAF

> *3¼ cups bread flour
> *1½ tablespoons dry milk
> *1½ teaspoons salt
> *2 tablespoons sugar
> 1 cup water
> 2 small eggs
> 1½ tablespoons butter
> 2 teaspoons dry yeast

If you are using this recipe to prepackage a mix of your own, pack the dry ingredients listed with an * and do not add remaining ingredients until you are ready to bake the bread.

DIRECTIONS: Place all the ingredients in the bread pan in the order recommended by the manufacturer. Program the machine for the white bread cycle, and bake the bread. When it has finished baking, remove the pan from the machine with potholders or oven mitts. Turn the bread pan upside down, and shake the loaf out of the pan. Place the bread on a wire rack to cool.

No-Fat-Added Bread

RECIPE FOR A ONE-POUND LOAF

   *2¼ cups bread flour
   *1 teaspoon salt
   *1 tablespoon dry milk
   *1 tablespoon sugar
   ⅞ cup water
   1¼ teaspoons dry yeast

If you are using this recipe to prepackage a mix of your own, pack the dry ingredients listed with an * and do not add remaining ingredients until you are ready to bake the bread.

RECIPE FOR A ONE-AND-ONE-HALF-POUND LOAF

*3¼ cups bread flour
*1½ tablespoons dry milk
*1½ teaspoons salt
*1½ tablespoons sugar
1⅜ cups water
1¾ teaspoons dry yeast

If you are using this recipe to prepackage a mix of your own, pack the dry ingredients listed with an * and do not add remaining ingredients until you are ready to bake the bread.

DIRECTIONS: Place all the ingredients in the bread pan in the order recommended by the manufacturer. Program the machine for the white bread cycle, and bake the bread. When it has finished baking, remove the pan from the machine with potholders or oven mitts. Turn the bread pan upside down, and shake the loaf out of the pan. Place the bread on a wire rack to cool.

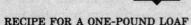

No-Salt-Added Bread

◆

RECIPE FOR A ONE-POUND LOAF

> *2¼ cups bread flour
> *1 tablespoon dry milk
> *1 tablespoon sugar
> ⅞ cup water
> 1 tablespoon butter or margarine
> 1 teaspoon dry yeast

If you are using this recipe to prepackage a mix of your own, pack the dry ingredients listed with an * and do not add remaining ingredients until you are ready to bake the bread.

RECIPE FOR A ONE-AND-ONE-HALF-POUND LOAF

> *3¼ cups bread flour
> *1½ tablespoons dry milk
> *1½ tablespoons sugar
> 1⅛ cups water
> 1½ tablespoons butter or margarine
> 1½ teaspoons dry yeast

If you are using this recipe to prepackage a mix of your own, pack the dry ingredients listed with an * and do not add remaining ingredients until you are ready to bake the bread.

DIRECTIONS: Place all the ingredients in the bread pan in the order recommended by the manufacturer. Program the machine for either the white or wheat bread cycle, and bake the bread. When it has finished baking, remove the pan from the machine with potholders or oven mitts. Turn the bread pan upside down, and shake the loaf out of the pan. Place the bread on a wire rack to cool.

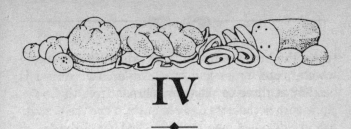

IV

◆

*Prepackaged Mixes
(or Simplifying Breadmaking)*

MAKE IT EVEN SIMPLER? YES, YOU CAN IF YOU
USE PREPACKAGED MIXES. Many prepackaged
mixes are available at your local supermarket.
When the objective is to create a loaf and not to
have to buy ingredients that you would not normally have on hand, they can be a great time and
money saver. Using prepackaged mixes may also
introduce you to flavors and types of bread that you
may never have tried before or would not be apt to
try from a recipe book.

You cannot make a mistake with a prepackaged
mix if you follow a few basic steps. A prepackaged
mix makes breadmaking even simpler since all you
need to do is open the package, pour the ingredients

into the bread pan, add approximately one cup of water, and press a button. *Voilà!* Your bread is ready in three to thirteen hours.

Using Prepackaged Mixes from Your Grocer's Shelf

There are wonderful prepackaged mixes in your grocery store with the number of brands and flavors continuously growing. The variety of mixes in the market ranges from the almost generic basic type to the gourmet brands. With every trip to the market, I am greeted by new mixes, flavors, and improved flavors. You will want to read the labels carefully to determine the ingredients used and whether the particular brand has additives, preservatives, or fats if these are of concern to you.

Some of my favorite basic bread mixes are made by Krusteaz under its Specialty Bread Mixes label. These mixes are sold in individual packages as well as in variety packages in a box. Both the flour mixes and the dry yeast are included. The Krusteaz varieties include primarily basic flavors, and the results consistently produced flavorful, well-risen breads.

The makers of Fleischmann's yeast make several varieties of bread mixes under the Dromedary Bakery label. They include basic white, stone ground wheat, sourdough, herb, and a delicious cheddar cheese. The Dromedary brands have no preservatives. They produce crisp and flavorful loaves with excellent texture. Pillsbury mixes come in basic flavors, including white and wheat, and are excellent bases for making your personalized additions. The Home Bakery brand did not consistently bake up well-risen loaves. They also did not turn out as flavorful in my machines. This could have been because of the machines in which I tested them or conditions in the kitchen, but everyone has personal preferences.

Then there are what I refer to as the gourmet mixes. In this category, cost does not always equate with quality or flavor. The most expensive prepared mixes I sampled from Sassafras Enterprises, Inc., for example, consistently made heavier, less flavorful loaves. I had great expectations when trying the Sassafras Honey Mustard Wheat Bread. Unfortunately it was a disappointment and lacked flavor and moisture.

There are an increasing number of companies out there with some incredibly delicious flavors and mixes. The outstanding mixes made by Dassant combine delicate flavor combinations, such as Danish Almond Poppyseed, Northwest Multigrain Honey, Farmhouse Oatmeal Wheat, Italian Garlic Basil, and Old Fashion Cinnamon Raisin, and create memorable flavored and textured breads. Even without any jam or butter, the slices of all the Dassant breads I baked seemed to melt in my mouth, tasting almost like a dessert. Danish Almond Poppyseed is my personal favorite.

Prepackaging Your Own Mixes Can Help You Create Wonderful Breads and Save You Time

You can derive some of the same time savings of using a prepackaged mix by making up several of your own. Breads from your own prepackaged mixes do not have to be dull or predictable. They can provide even more interesting flavors, variety, and taste treats than the store-bought prepackaged mixes. If you utilize a combination of store-bought and homemade prepackaged mixes and constantly try a variety of new recipes, you will be able to achieve great versatility with your bread machine.

How to Prepackage Your Own Mixes

When you decide to prepackage your own mixes, you will have quality, flavor, and ingredient control and will fill your refrigerator and pantry with the necessary mix to prepare a loaf of bread in less than three minutes. You need to find a recipe that works well in your machine and is a simple combination of ingredients. Start with your bread machine manufacturer's basic wheat or white bread or the Basic White or Basic Wheat Combo Bread recipes in the preceding chapter. If you love the bread from these recipes, you are now ready to prepare several prepackaged mixes of your own. If these recipes do not have you thinking about tasting the next loaf, try some other basic recipes from cookbooks, magazines, or friends until you find your personal favorites. Once you select one or two, you can pre-measure all the dry ingredients except the yeast for several loaves at a time rather than just for one loaf.

Instructions for Prepackaged Mixes, Six at a Time

Although any number of mixes can be made, preparing six at a time is manageable and not too time-consuming.

Have enough dry ingredients on hand to make at least six loaves. You will need six one-half-gallon plastic zipper-lock bags and six containers (bowls or pans) large enough to hold four cups of ingredients. To make the mixes, follow these easy steps:

1. Set out the plastic bags.
2. Set out the six bowls on your kitchen counter.
3. Measure the dry ingredients so each bowl or pan has the correct measured amount of ingredients to make one loaf of bread. In the first bowl or pan, start with the flour (usually the first ingredient in

the recipe), and measure the amount called for in the recipe. Place it in the first bowl. Then measure an equal amount of flour, and place it in each of the remaining five bowls or pans. When you have completed measuring flour, you should have six bowls each containing the amount of flour necessary to make one loaf of bread.

Continue with the next ingredient in the recipe necessary to make one bread, and place that amount in each bowl or pan. For example, measure the dry milk for each container.

Continue with the remaining ingredients until all dry ingredients except the yeast are in the bowls. Include salt and sugar or any other dry ingredient except for the yeast. Remember, do not measure or add the yeast to the dry mix at this time.

4. Place the ingredients from each bowl or pan in a plastic bag, and seal the bag. Make sure the bag is dry before you put the dry ingredients in it. You may write on each bag the type of bread mix and the date you prepared it. Bags may be reused to prepackage more mixes.

5. Keep the mixes in a refrigerator or freezer until you are ready to use them.

When it is time to make a bread, remove an individual bag from the freezer or refrigerator. Let it sit until it reaches room temperature. Then pour the flour/dry mixture from one plastic bag into the bread machine baking pan, add the water and the fat, and place the dry yeast in either the top yeast dispenser or on top of the flour in the bread machine pan.

By using these prepackaged mixes, you can cut the time and eliminate any small potential mess of measuring flour when you are in a hurry. The great thing about using your own prepackaged mixes is that they will become a base for personalized breads with a minimum of effort.

Ways to Personalize Your Breadmaking with Prepackaged Mixes

No one would ever guess that the following additions and suggestions for prepackaged mixes could make interesting and delicious breads every time, but they can! Here are some ways to personalize your breads. Prepackaged mixes will be transformed into specialty breads when you add one or two ingredients at the end of the first kneading or to the dry ingredients once they are in the bread pan just before you add the liquid. Consider adding one-half cup of applesauce; one-half mashed ripe banana; one-half cup of chocolate chips; one-quarter to one-half cup of chopped dried fruits; one-quarter to one-half cup of chopped nuts; three tablespoons of peanut butter; one-half cup of grated cheese; one to two tablespoons of dried spices or herbs; or the

contents of one-half to one package of a vegetable
or onion soup mix as included in the recipe for Onion
Soup Mix Bread in Chapter V, page 83.

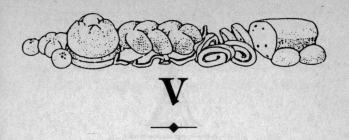

V

◆

A–Z Recipes and Ideas

In this chapter you will find out the secrets of how to take common ingredients and come up with spectacular results. The suggestions and special recipes in this chapter were selected after hundreds of taste tests by neighbors, friends, relatives, and associates who helped determine which recipes are special.

Apples

Apples and bread are a natural combination. This is because the sweetness and moisture that apples bring to the bread can be the basis for other spices or fruits, including cinnamon, dried raisins, cherries, or cranberries.

Apple Bread Recipe

Start with any basic white or wheat bread recipe, the Basic White or Basic Wheat Combo Bread recipe in this book or a prepackaged homemade or store-bought mix. Then make the following substitution: For the one-pound loaf, replace all the water with ⅞ cup applesauce. Add ½ teaspoon cinnamon and ¼ teaspoon nutmeg to the dry ingredients. For the one-and-one-half-pound loaf, replace all the water with 1¼ cups applesauce. Add 1 teaspoon cinnamon and ¼ teaspoon nutmeg to the dry ingredients. You may also add raisins or other dried fruits in small pieces to the dry ingredients, after the first kneading or according to the manufacturer's recommendation on when to make additions.

Apple Juice as a Sweetener

To sweeten any loaf without adding sugar, replace one-half the water in the recipe with apple juice.

Apple Pie Filling as a Substitute for Water

Apple pie filling combines chunks of apples with a sweet base. Substitute an equal amount of canned apple pie filling for water or the liquid ingredients in any bread recipe to create a bread that is moist, sweet, and delicious toasted.

Applesauce as a Fat Substitute

To eliminate fat in white or wheat bread recipes, replace the amount of fat called for with the same amount of applesauce. Bread made with applesauce is particularly great for peanut butter and jelly sandwiches. When applesauce is substituted for fat, the one to three tablespoons of applesauce do not drastically change the taste of the bread.

The texture of a bread made with applesauce instead of butter is slightly more mealy (not quite as elastic) and the crust is not as crispy.

B

Bagels

"Do they really taste like, you know, real bagels?" was the question friends asked before they tasted the homemade bagels out of my oven. The answer was "Yes, but better." By making your own bagels, you can ensure hot bagels right out of the oven, crusty on the outside, soft on the inside, with your favorite toppings of poppy seeds, salt, onion, cheese, or sesame seeds.

Homemade Bagel Recipe (Makes 8)

◆

2 cups bread flour
¾ cup water
1 teaspoon salt
1½ tablespoons sugar
1½ teaspoons dry yeast
½ teaspoon any of the following: poppy
  seeds, sesame seeds, coarse salt,
  onion powder, Parmesan cheese,
  caraway seeds

Place all ingredients in your bread machine pan in the order recommended by the manufacturer's directions. Prepare the ingredients using the dough cycle on your machine. When the dough is ready, remove it from the bread pan and place it on a floured board.

Forming the bagels: Divide the dough into eight pieces. Prepare each bagel by taking one piece of dough and rolling it between your hands or on the floured board to make a rope approximately 1? to 14 inches long. Take the two ends of the rope, and pinch them together into a circle. Place it on the board. Repeat with each piece of dough until eight bagels are formed. Let the bagels rest on the board for 5 to 10 minutes.

Boiling the bagels: Bring 2 quarts water in a large pan on the stove to a boil. Add 1 tablespoon molasses or sugar to the boiling water. After the dough has rested 5 to 10 minutes, with a slotted spoon place each bagel in the boiling water until it rises to the top of the water. Turn each bagel, leaving it in the water for 2 to 3 seconds more. Remove each bagel from the water with the slotted spoon, drain the excess water and immediately place the bagel on a greased baking sheet.

Accessorizing and baking the bagels: After all eight bagels have been boiled, sprinkle each with any combination of your favorite toppings, including, but not limited to, ½ teaspoon poppy seeds or sesame seeds, coarse (kosher) salt, onion powder, Parmesan cheese, or caraway seeds. Bake in a preheated 375-degree oven for 20 to 25 minutes, or until golden brown. Remove the pan from the oven. Cool the bagels on a wire rack.

Broccoli

Broccoli florets along with sliced olives lend a Mediterranean flavor to a wheat or white bread.

Broccoli Olive Bread Recipe

◆

To your favorite white or wheat bread recipe, the Basic White or Basic Wheat Combo Bread recipe in this book, or to a prepackaged homemade or store-bought mix add ¼ cup chopped black olives and ½ cup very small pieces washed and dried broccoli florets. If possible, add the olives and broccoli to the machine after the first kneading or according to the manufacturer's recommendation on when to make additions. Place all the ingredients in the bread pan in the order recommended by the manufacturer. Program the machine for the white or wheat bread cycle, and bake the bread. When it has finished baking, remove the pan from the machine with potholders or oven mitts. Turn the bread pan upside down, and shake the loaf out of the pan. Place the bread on a wire rack to cool.

C

Cake Mixes

S ome bread machines have quick bread features
(the Zojirushi and large Panasonic models are
two that do). Your bread machine can make an excellent pound cake with an ordinary cake mix. Mix
the ingredients in a mixing bowl, add them to the
bread machine pan, and then bake the cake on
the quick bread cycle according to the directions
of the manufacturer. Open the lid of the machine
after the quick bread cycle has concluded, and use
a toothpick to test for doneness. If the toothpick
inserted into the cake comes out dry, remove the
bread pan with potholders or oven mitts, and turn
the cake onto a cooling rack. When it is completely

cool, frost it and enjoy! For the rare time when the toothpick does not come out dry (this may occur when you are making a very heavy cake batter recipe), complete baking the loaf in your oven. Turn on your oven to 350 degrees. Using potholders or oven mitts, place the bread machine pan in a square or oblong baking pan to prevent its tipping. Place the baking pan in your oven, and continue baking until the toothpick comes out dry. Test it every 10 minutes. Usually, after 10 to 20 minutes the unfinished cake will be done.

Streusel Cake Mix

To make a streusel cake from a mix in your bread machine, start with a streusel cake mix, and prepare the batter in a bowl according to the directions on the box. When the batter is mixed, pour it into the bread machine pan. Sprinkle ½ the streusel topping into the batter in the pan. Stir it gently with a spoon to mix the streusel into the batter. Pour the remaining streusel mixture on top of the batter, and bake it according to the manufacturer's instructions. When the cake has finished baking, remove it from the pan from the machine with potholders or oven mitts. Turn the pan upside down, and shake the cake out of the pan. Place the cake on a wire rack to cool.

Cheese Breads

Cheese breads offer a variety of textures, colors, and flavors for experimenting and eating. Think about eating your favorite grilled cheese sandwich or tuna on cheddar, mozzarella, or Swiss cheese bread.

To make a cheese bread, add ½ to 1 cup grated cheese to the dry ingredients of any white or wheat bread recipe, the Basic White or Basic Wheat Combo recipe in this book, or a prepackaged home-made or store-bought mix. Sharper types of cheese will return their flavor more than mild ones. When you add cheese to bread, it is necessary to reduce the fat in the bread recipe by half, and you should be ready for the loaf to rise less than a loaf without cheese. Make your bread according to the particular instructions of the recipe you choose.

Mozzarella Cheese and Sun-Dried Tomato Bread Recipe (with Black Olive Option)

◆

This is a great accompaniment to a pasta dinner!

Recipe for a One-Pound Loaf

2 cups bread flour
½ teaspoon salt
1 tablespoon sugar
1 tablespoon olive oil
½ cup chopped sun-dried tomatoes
½ cup water
1½ teaspoons dry yeast
½ cup shredded mozzarella cheese
¼ cup sliced black olives (optional)

Recipe for a One-and-One-Half-Pound Loaf

3 cups bread flour
1 teaspoon salt
1½ tablespoons sugar
1½ tablespoons olive oil
¾ cup chopped sun-dried tomatoes
¾ cup water
2¼ teaspoons dry yeast
⅝ cup shredded mozzarella cheese
½ cup sliced black olives (optional)

DIRECTIONS: Place all the ingredients except the mozzarella cheese in the bread pan in the order recommended by the manufacturer. Bake the bread on the white bread cycle. Add the mozzarella cheese and sliced black olives (optional) at the end of the first kneading or according to the manufacturer's recommendation on when to make additions. When the bread cycle is complete, take the bread out of the machine with potholders or oven mitts. Turn the bread pan upside down, and shake the loaf out of pan. Place the bread on a wire rack to cool.

Chocolate Chip

C hocolate chips go well with just about anything as far as I am concerned. This Chocolate Chip Bread is a real treat for chocolate lovers.

Chocolate Chip Bread Recipe

◆

Start with any basic white or wheat bread recipe, the Basic White or Basic Wheat Combo Bread recipe in this book, or a prepackaged homemade or store-bought mix. Add ⅓ cup chocolate chips (I prefer the very small ones) to the dry mixture. Place the ingredients in the bread pan in the order recommended by the manufacturer. Program the machine for the white or wheat bread cycle, and bake the bread. When it has finished baking, remove the pan from the machine with potholders or oven mitts.

Turn the bread pan upside down, and shake the loaf out of the pan. Place the bread on a wire rack to cool. The results will be either a swirled chocolate bread or, on occasion, a completely chocolate bread.

Note: To keep chocolate chips from melting, freeze them for approximately 1 hour before adding them to the ingredients. If you are not using the timer and want to ensure that the chocolate chips will not melt, wait to add them until after the first kneading or according to the manufacturer's recommendation on when to make additions.

Coffee Cake

This specialty is often similar in taste to a sweet, fragrant bread.

Special Coffee Cake Bread with Dried Fruit Recipe

———◆———

This is richer and sweeter than most other breads. Plain or toasted it is outstanding.

RECIPE FOR A ONE-POUND LOAF

    2¾ cups bread flour
    ½ teaspoon salt
    5 tablespoons sugar
    5 tablespoons butter (cut into ½-inch
      pieces)
    2 eggs
    6 tablespoons water
    2½ teaspoons dry yeast
    ½ cup dried fruit, such as chopped
      dates or apricots, dried cherries,
      blueberries, or cranberries
    ⅓ cup chopped nuts, such as walnuts
      or pecans (if desired)

Recipe for a One-and-One-Half-Pound Loaf

3½ cups bread flour
1 teaspoon salt
½ cup sugar
¼ pound (1 stick = 8 tablespoons) butter
  (cut into ½-inch pieces)
3 eggs
½ cup water
1 tablespoon dry yeast
⅔ cup dried fruit, such as dried dates
  or apricots, dried cherries,
  blueberries, or cranberries
⅓ cup chopped nuts, such as walnuts
  or pecans (if desired)

DIRECTIONS: Place all the ingredients except the dried fruit in the machine according to the manufacturer's instructions. Bake the bread on the white bread cycle. Add the chopped fruit after the first kneading or according to the manufacturer's recommendation on when to make additions. When the baking is complete, remove the bread pan from the machine with potholders or oven mitts. Turn the pan upside down, and shake out the loaf. Place the bread on a wire rack to cool.

Croutons

To use up leftover bread, cut it into ¾-inch slices, then crosswise into cubes. Place the bread cubes in a glass or metal pan. Sprinkle them with 1 to 2 tablespoons olive oil or butter, then with your favorite herb or spice. (Suggested herbs and spices are garlic, dill, oregano, and basil.) Bake in a preheated 350-degree oven for 20 minutes. When the croutons are crispy, remove the pan from the oven with oven mitts or potholders. Let the croutons cool, and then use them on salads, or in soups.

To store croutons, place them in a plastic bag and keep them in a dry place. You may even freeze them for later use. When you are ready to use them, defrost the croutons at room temperature for 5 minutes before serving.

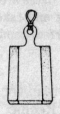

D

Dates

C hopped or whole dates are a welcome addition to many breads and cakes. Date Nut Pecan Bread blends the perfect combination of nuts and fruit.

Date Nut Pecan Bread (or Date Nut Bread) Recipe

◆

Start with any basic white or wheat bread recipe, the Basic White or Basic Wheat Combo Bread recipe in this book, or a prepackaged homemade or store-bought mix. Add to the dry ingredients ⅓ cup chopped dates and ⅓ cup chopped pecans or walnuts. Add the liquid ingredients, and bake the bread according to the manufacturer's instructions. For a richer date nut loaf, substitute 1 whole egg for a portion of the water or milk in the liquid ingredients. To do this, place an egg in a measuring cup and fill it with water or milk until the liquid reaches the amount called for in the recipe. Place the ingredients in the bread pan in the order recommended by the manufacturer. Program the machine for the white or wheat bread cycle, and bake the bread. When it has finished baking, remove the pan from the machine with potholders or oven mitts. Turn the bread pan upside down, and shake the loaf out of the pan. Place the bread on a wire rack to cool.

Dill

Dried or fresh dill is a delicate yet flavorful herb and can be added to wheat, white, or your favorite egg bread.

Dill Egg Bread Recipe

◆

Starting with your favorite egg bread recipe, add 2 tablespoons freshly washed, chopped dill or 1 tablespoon dried dill to the dry ingredients. Place all the ingredients in the bread pan in the order recommended by the manufacturer. Program the machine for the white bread cycle, and bake the bread. When it has finished baking, remove the pan from the machine with potholders or oven mitts. Turn the bread pan upside down, and shake the loaf out of the pan. Place the bread on a wire rack to cool. The addition of dill creates a bread that is a terrific accompaniment to salads or fish dishes. Leftover dill bread makes outstanding croutons.

E

Eggs

To use or not use eggs in bread recipes depends on your diet as well as the recipes. Many recipes add eggs merely to make a loaf richer, while for coffee cake bread recipes, the egg is an integral part of the texture of the loaf. In basic bread recipes, you can omit the egg as long as you substitute a like amount of liquid. In specialty doughs, such as coffee cakes and rich breads, the results could change drastically if you omit the eggs.

Focaccia

Similar to pizza dough without all the toppings, focaccia is a perfect accompaniment to a meal of spaghetti, pasta, or soup. Create your own toppings by choosing from such spices and herbs as basil, thyme, and oregano and from garnishes like sliced olives, dried shredded tomatoes, chopped onions, or Parmesan cheese.

Focaccia Recipe (1 large or 2 medium flat breads)

◆

1 cup water
2 tablespoons olive oil (or any
    vegetable oil)
½ to 1 teaspoon salt
2½ cups bread flour
1½ teaspoons dry yeast
2 tablespoons olive oil for sprinkling
    on bread before baking
optional: ¼ to ½ cup Parmesan cheese
oregano, basil, or thyme leaves for
    flavor

DIRECTIONS: Add all the ingredients to the bread machine pan according to the order suggested by the manufacturer. Set the machine on the dough cycle, and prepare the dough. When it is done, remove it from the bread machine pan, and set it on a floured board. Cover the dough with a damp towel, and allow it to rest for 10 to 15 minutes.

Either make 1 bread or divide the dough in half and make 2 medium-size breads. (Whichever size you make, the basic procedure is the same.) Roll out the dough on the floured board with a rolling pin until the dough is anywhere from ¼ to ⅜ inch thick (the thickness can vary according to personal taste). After the dough has been rolled out, transfer it to a greased baking pan. Sprinkle each bread with 1 to 2 tablespoons olive oil. Now sprinkle the dough with your choice of fresh or dry oregano, basil, or thyme leaves. Also sprinkle it with ¼ to ½ cup Parmesan cheese, if desired. Bake the focaccia for 15 to 25 minutes in a preheated 350-degree oven, or until golden brown. Remove the focaccia from the oven and serve it warm.

Fruit

Any white or wheat bread, the Basic White or Wheat Combo Bread in this book, or any pre-packaged homemade or store-bought bread is livened up with the addition of fruit. The fruit can be fresh, canned, or dried.

When you use fresh fruits, chop ½ cup of the desired fruit, and add it to the dry ingredients before mixing in the liquid ingredients. You may add canned fruit in the same way as fresh, but you should thoroughly drain the fruit before you add it. (If you include the juice from the canned fruit, reduce the liquid called for in the recipe by a like amount of the added juice.) For dried fruits, carefully chop ¼ to ½ cup of the desired fruit, and for best results, add it to the bread mixture whenever the manufacturer recommends you add ingredients. If the dried fruit is added directly to the dry ingredients, the bread will still taste like the added fruit, but the pieces will be mashed in by the mixing blade.

G

Grape Juice

Grape juice, preferably white, can be substituted for a part of the water in a bread recipe when you wish to make a sweeter bread. At most, substitute half the water called for with the grape juice.

H

Herb Bread

Herbs and spices can be added to any basic recipe. Remember when you use dry herbs, such as oregano, basil, verbena, etc., you should be sure to add only 1 teaspoon to 1 tablespoon. When fresh herbs are used, up to 2 or 3 tablespoons of the chopped fresh herbs can be added. Other herbs and spices that make interesting breads include parsley, chives, marjoram, thyme, nutmeg, rosemary, tarragon, and cilantro.

Honey

Honey is a wonderful substitute for sugar in many of your favorite recipes. Replace the sugar with equal amounts of honey. Some baking sources recommend varying the amount when honey is used, but I have found that an even substitution works just fine.

A sweet breakfast coffee cake–like bread is a Honey Apricot Walnut Loaf, which is sweetened with both honey and brown sugar.

Honey Apricot Walnut Loaf Recipe

RECIPE FOR A ONE-POUND LOAF

   4 tablespoons honey
   2 tablespoons butter
   ⅝ cup milk
   1 egg
   1½ teaspoons vanilla
   1½ cups bread flour
   ½ teaspoon salt
   2 tablespoons brown sugar
   ¼ cup chopped apricots
   ¼ cup chopped walnuts
   1½ teaspoons dry yeast

RECIPE FOR A ONE-AND-ONE-HALF-POUND LOAF

¼ cup plus 1 tablespoon honey
3 tablespoons butter
1 cup milk
2 eggs
2 teaspoons vanilla
2½ cups bread flour
¾ teaspoon salt
3 tablespoons brown sugar
⅓ cup chopped apricots
½ chopped walnuts
2½ teaspoons dry yeast

DIRECTIONS: In a small saucepan on your stove over low heat, warm the honey, butter, and milk until the butter is melted. Remove the mixture from the heat, and allow it to cool to lukewarm. Add the eggs, vanilla, flour, and salt, and the honey mixture to your bread machine. Place the ingredients in the bread pan in the order recommended by the manufacturer. Set the machine for white bread, and start the cycle. Add the brown sugar, apricots, and walnuts at the end of the first kneading or according to the manufacturer's recommendation on when to make additions. With a plastic spatula or spoon, stir the ingredients gently into the flour mixture in the bread pan, making sure that large clumps of flour do not stick to the sides or the bottom of the bread pan. Be sure not to scratch the pan. Close the lid, and continue baking the bread until the baking cycle is complete. When the bread has finished baking, remove the pan from the machine with potholders or oven mitts. Turn the bread pan upside down, and shake the loaf out of the pan. Place the bread on a wire rack to cool.

J

Jam

When you have an abundance of strawberries, apricots, or peaches and your bread machine has a jam-making option, try either this Summer Fresh Fruit Jam recipe or the one suggested by the manufacturer of your machine. Cleanup will be easy, and the stove does not have to be turned on. Because directions vary with each manufacturer, be sure to consult those of your machine's manufacturer. Refrigerate the jam, and use it up within one week. THIS RECIPE MAY BE MADE ONLY IN A BREAD MACHINE WITH A JAM MAKER OPTION.

Summer Fresh Fruit Jam Recipe
(Makes 1 cup)

◆

2 cups of one of the following fresh
fruits
  Blueberries: wash and measure
  Strawberries: remove stems and
    hulls, and cut into quarters
  Peaches and apricots: Set in hot
    water; remove the skins and pits;
    cut into 2-inch pieces
½ cup sugar
1 to 2 tablespoons lemon juice

DIRECTIONS: Pour the prepared fruit into the bread pan; sprinkle the sugar over the fruit, and add the lemon juice. Let the mixture rest for 2 to 3 minutes. Set the machine for the jam cycle, and start. When the jam is done, remove it from the pan, and pour it into a plastic or glass container. Let the jam cool; then put it in the refrigerator. Wash out the bread pan immediately with soapy warm water. The jam will thicken in the refrigerator.

L

Leftover Fruits and Vegetables

Add ⅓ to ½ cup well-drained chopped fruits or vegetables to the dry ingredients in your bread machine. When the fruits or vegetables are especially moist, compensate by reducing the liquid in the recipe by 1 to 2 tablespoons.

Lemon Zest

The addition of delicate lemon zest to a bread makes a plain white bread a teatime favorite. Lemon zest and poppy seeds turn white or wheat bread into Lemon Poppy Seed Bread.

Lemon Poppy Seed Bread Recipe

---◆---

Grate the zest of 1 lemon, and add it and 2 table-spoons poppy seeds to the dry ingredients of your favorite basic white or wheat bread recipe, the Basic White Bread or Basic Wheat Combo Bread recipe in this book, or to a prepackaged homemade or store-bought mix. This recipe is just as delicious if you eliminate all added fat from the ingredients. Place all the ingredients in the bread pan in the order recommended by the manufacturer. Program the machine for the white or wheat bread cycle, and bake the bread. When it has finished baking, remove the pan from the machine with potholders or oven mitts. Turn the bread pan upside down, and shake the loaf out of the pan. Place the bread on a wire rack to cool.

Nuts

Nuts contribute a wonderful flavor to most breads if you remember a few basic tips. Do not add more than ⅓ cup unless the recipe specifically calls for more. Chop the nuts into ¼-inch to ½-inch pieces. If you are not using the automatic timer feature on your machine, add the nuts after the first kneading so they will not mash too much.

O

Oatmeal

Add 3 tablespoons of uncooked oatmeal to the dry ingredients of any bread recipe. In addition, increase the liquid in the recipe by 1 tablespoon.

Onion Soup Mix

Use onion soup mix in your bread machine to make an Onion Soup Mix Bread.

Onion Soup Mix Bread Recipe

◆

Start with any basic white or wheat bread recipe, the Basic White or Basic Wheat Combo Bread recipe in this book, or a prepackaged homemade or store-bought mix. After all the dry ingredients have been measured, bring the amount of water called for in the recipe to a boil, and add it to a package of onion soup mix. When this mixture has cooled slightly, add it to the dry ingredients. (It is strictly a matter of taste whether to add part or all of the soup package. An entire package may be added to either the one-pound or the one-and-one-half-pound loaf.) Place all the ingredients in the bread pan in the order recommended by the manufacturer. Program the machine for the white or wheat bread cycle, and bake the bread. When it has finished baking, remove the pan from the machine with potholders or oven mitts. Turn the bread pan upside down, and shake the loaf out of the pan. Place the bread on a wire rack to cool.

P

Peanut Butter

Use peanut butter with chocolate chips in a bread? Wake me, I must be dreaming!

Peanut Butter Chocolate Chip Bread Recipe I

Start with any white or wheat bread recipe, the Basic White or Basic Wheat Combo Bread recipe in this book, or a prepackaged homemade or store-bought mix. Add 3 tablespoons smooth or chunky peanut butter and ½ cup chocolate chips to the dry ingredients. Place all the ingredients in the bread pan in the order recommended by the manufacturer. Program the machine for the white or wheat bread cycle, and bake the bread. When it has finished baking, remove the pan from the machine with potholders or oven mitts. Turn the bread pan upside down and shake the loaf out of the pan. Place the bread on a wire rack to cool. The texture of this bread will be heavier than most, but children of all ages will love the aroma and flavor. *Note:* To prevent chocolate from melting during baking (which would result in a chocolate or a chocolate swirl bread), freeze the chocolate chips for approximately 1 hour before you add them. Also, if you are not using the automatic timer, add the chocolate chips after the first kneading or according to the manufacturer's recommendation on when to make additions.

Peanut Butter Chocolate Chip Bread
Recipe II

---◆---

Here oat bran adds texture to make a denser loaf. Banana slices on pieces of Peanut Butter Chocolate Chip Bread II are a delight.

RECIPE FOR A ONE-POUND LOAF

    2 cups plus 1 tablespoon bread flour
    3 tablespoons oat bran
    2 tablespoons dry milk
    3 tablespoons sugar
    ½ teaspoon salt
    6 tablespoons peanut butter (smooth or
       chunky)
    ⅞ cup water
    1½ teaspoons dry yeast
    ½ cup chocolate chips

RECIPE FOR A ONE-AND-ONE-HALF-POUND LOAF

    3 cups plus 2 tablespoons bread flour
    4 tablespoons oat bran
    3 tablespoons dry milk
    ¼ cup sugar
    1 teaspoon salt
    ½ cup peanut butter (smooth or
       chunky)
    1¼ cups water
    2¼ teaspoons dry yeast
    ¾ cup chocolate chips

DIRECTIONS: Add all the ingredients except the chocolate chips to the bread machine. Set your machine on the white bread cycle, and begin baking. Add the chocolate chips after the first kneading or according to the manufacturer's recommendation on when to make additions. When the bread has finished baking, remove the pan from the machine with potholders or oven mitts. Turn the pan upside down, and shake the loaf out of the pan. Place the bread on a wire rack to cool.

Note: In this recipe you may also freeze the chocolate chips for at least 1 hour before using to prevent them from melting.

Pizza—California Style

This kind of pizza does not even compare with your local restaurant pizza. It is so much better! Use your favorite combination of vegetables and toppings, along with regular, low-fat, or no-fat mozzarella cheese to make refreshing and delicious Pizza California Style. The ingredients in the pizza dough are plain and simple, but the pizza is anything but that.

PIZZA CALIFORNIA STYLE RECIPE
(1 large [13" x 9"] or 2 medium [9" x 9" round] pizzas)

⅔ cup water
1½ tablespoons olive oil (or vegetable oil)
½ teaspoon salt
2 cups bread flour
1½ teaspoons dry yeast
1–1½ cups mozzarella cheese, shredded
½–1 cup chopped tomato (or 1 cup tomato sauce)
vegetables (mushrooms, green pepper, olives, broccoli) cut into ¼"–⅓" thin slices
Oregano, basil, pepper

DIRECTIONS: Add all the ingredients to the bread machine pan in the order recommended by the manufacturer. Set the machine on the dough function and start it. When the cycle is complete, remove the dough from the bread pan, and place it on a floured board. Decide whether you want to make 1 large or 2 medium pizzas.

For two pizzas divide the dough in half. Roll out two 9" circles or 9" x 9" squares, using the floured board and a rolling pin with a small amount of flour to prevent sticking. For one rectangular or round pizza, roll out the entire piece of dough to fit the

pan. Place the dough in a greased pan (spray shortening works well). Press the dough to the corners
of the pan(s).

Top each pizza with at least 1–1½ cups mozzarella
cheese, shredded. Add ½ to 1 cup chopped tomato
(or 1 cup tomato sauce). Now add your favorite
chopped vegetables, including thinly sliced mushrooms; ¼-to-⅛-inch chopped green peppers;
pimento-stuffed sliced olives; and/or broccoli florets
cut into small pieces. Sprinkle oregano, basil, and
pepper on the top of the dough. You may include
meat such as thin ham slices or ½ to 1 cup cooked
chopped meat.

Bake the pizza(s) in preheated 425-degree oven
for 15 to 25 minutes, or until the crust is golden
brown. Remove the pizza(s) from the oven with
oven mitts or potholders. Cut the pizza(s) into
regular-size slices or into bite-size pieces for appetizers. Serve immediately.

Pretzels, Soft

Similar in texture to soft sweet rolls, soft pretzels are an excellent snack or a way for children to help create their own snacks. Although
shaping pretzels is much easier to do than to de-
scribe, you need to experiment a few times to come
up with the correct shape. The next time you are
at the grocery store or are eating a pretzel in your

home, pay attention to the shape, so you can duplicate it when you make your own soft pretzels.

Soft Pretzels Recipe (Makes 8)

◆

2 cups bread flour
¼ to ½ teaspoon salt
1 tablespoon sugar
½ cup water
1 egg

FOR TOPPING:

Coarse (kosher) salt
One egg yolk
Poppy seeds or sesame seeds (optional)

DIRECTIONS: Place all the ingredients except the egg yolk, coarse salt, and optional poppy seeds or sesame seeds in the bread machine pan in the order recommended by the manufacturer. Set the machine on the dough function, and start it. When the dough is done, remove it from the bread pan, and place it on a floured board. Divide the dough into eight pieces. Form each piece into a 12″ to 14″ rope by rolling it either between your two hands or on the floured board with a floured rolling pin.

To form the rope into a pretzel, find its center; this will be the bottom point of a heart. Cross the two ends at the top, leaving each piece 3 inches long after they are twisted around each other. The pretzel now looks like a heart with the top center having two-inch pieces extending. Pinch the remaining two 3-inch pieces onto the bottom sides of the heart. The traditional look of a pretzel will emerge as you shape it.

Once your eight pretzels are formed, place them on a greased baking sheet. Beat the egg yolk, and paint some on each pretzel with the back of a teaspoon or pastry brush. Then sprinkle each pretzel lightly with coarse salt. You may also sprinkle the pretzels with poppy seeds, sesame seeds, or other toppings as you desire.

Bake the pretzels in a 375-degree preheated oven for 15 to 20 minutes, or until golden brown. When the pretzels are done, remove the pan from the oven with oven mitts or potholders. Remove the pretzels from the pan with a spatula, and place them on a wire rack to cool.

Rolls and Breadsticks and Twists

These are as easy as one, two, three to make when your bread machine prepares the dough.

Rolls and Breadsticks and Twists Recipe

—◆—

1. MAKE THE DOUGH

Using the dough cycle on your machine, make either a white or wheat bread dough, using the Basic White or Wheat Combo recipe in this book, or use a prepackaged homemade or store-

bought mix. *When the machine indicates the dough is ready, remove it from the machine, push out the gas, and get ready to shape the dough into rolls and breadsticks. Divide 1 pound of dough into twelve balls. Divide 1½ pounds of dough into eighteen balls. Spray the balls with a mist of water, and cover them with a damp kitchen towel. Let them rest for 15 to 20 minutes on your counter in the kitchen.*

2. SHAPE THE DOUGH

Rolls: To shape the dough for rolls, form each ball into either a round shape or an oval. For brioche-shaped rolls, break off a small piece (the size of a hazelnut) of dough, and shape both the small and large pieces into balls. Set the small ball on top of the large one, pressing it into place. Put the rolls on a greased baking sheet. Sprinkle the tops with poppy seeds, sesame seeds, salt, garlic or onion powder, or herbs. Cover the sheet. Let the rolls rise until they are doubled in size.

Breadsticks: To make breadsticks, roll a ball of dough between your hands to make an eight-inch rope. Now roll each rope in poppy seeds, salt, or garlic or onion powder before placing it on a greased baking tin. Place a moistened cloth over the dough, and allow it to rise out of the way of any drafts until it is doubled in size.

Twists: Follow the same procedure as for breadsticks, except make two thinner eight-inch ropes with each ball. Twist the two rope pieces together. Let rise as for breadsticks.

3. BAKE THE DOUGH

Bake in a preheated 350-degree oven for 10 to 15 minutes, or until brown. Remove the baking pan from the oven with oven mitts or potholders. Place the rolls, breadsticks, or twists on a wire rack to cool.

S

Spices and Herbs

Add spices or herbs to the dry ingredients of any white, wheat, or egg bread. Just 1 teaspoon of cinnamon can turn a white bread into a cinnamon loaf; 1 tablespoon of dried or 2 tablespoons of fresh dill will create an herb loaf. Recently a friend brought dried lemon verbena for me to test. Adding 1 tablespoon of crushed lemon verbena to the Lemon Poppy Seed Bread was fantastic. See the recipe in this chapter for Lemon Poppy Seed Bread (page 80).

Spinach

Spinach combined with feta cheese makes not only great appetizers and spinach pies but also spectacular bread. Spinach Feta Cheese Bread can be eaten plain. When is a tomato sandwich not just a tomato sandwich? When it is made with Spinach Feta Cheese Bread and sliced fresh tomatoes from your garden. It then becomes a tomato sandwich beyond compare!

Spinach Feta Cheese Bread Recipe

RECIPE FOR A ONE-POUND LOAF

⅓ cup crumbled feta cheese
2 tablespoons olive oil
¾ teaspoon salt
2¼ cups bread flour
½ cup well-drained defrosted spinach
(or well-washed spinach)
2 teaspoons sugar
⅓ cup water
1 egg
½ teaspoon ground nutmeg
¼ teaspoon pepper
1½ teaspoons dry yeast

RECIPE FOR A ONE-AND-ONE-HALF-POUND LOAF

½ cup crumbled feta cheese
3 tablespoons olive oil
1 teaspoon salt
3⅓ cups bread flour
¾ cup well-drained defrosted spinach
   (or well-washed fresh spinach)
1 tablespoon sugar
½ cup water
1 egg
¾ teaspoon ground nutmeg
½ teaspoon pepper
2 teaspoons dry yeast

DIRECTIONS: Add all the ingredients to the bread pan in the order recommended by the manufacturer. Program the machine for the white bread cycle. When the bread has finished baking, remove the pan from the machine with potholders or oven mitts. Turn the bread pan upside down, and shake the loaf out of the pan. Place the bread on a wire rack to cool.

T

Tomatoes

Fresh, sun-dried, or in bits, tomatoes supply color and flavor to breads.

Chopped seeded tomatoes (¼ to ½ cup) can be added to dry ingredients for white or wheat bread before it is baked. To use sun-dried tomatoes in any bread recipe, chop up to 3 tablespoons of sun-dried tomatoes and add them to the dry ingredients.

Recently in the spice section of the grocery store I discovered tomato flakes. I sprinkled 1 tablespoon of the dried flakes into the dry ingredients for a white bread. The tomato flakes produced a similar taste to that of sun-dried tomatoes but were easier to use. When using chopped, dried, or flaked tomatoes, bake the following bread recipe after you have added the tomatoes to the dry ingredients. When the bread has finished baking, remove the pan from the machine with potholders or oven mitts. Turn the bread pan upside down, and a shake the loaf out of the pan. Place the bread on a wire rack to cool.

V

Vegetable Soup Mix (Dry)

Vegetable soup mix added to the dry ingredients for any white or wheat bread makes a bread that is a perfect accompaniment for soups or stews.

Vegetable Soup Bread Recipe

◆

Start with the basic recipe for white or wheat bread, the Basic White or Basic Wheat Combo bread in this book, or a prepackaged homemade or store-bought mix. Before adding the water to the dry mixture, bring it to a boil. Add 1 full package of dried vegetable soup mix to the water. Let this mixture sit for approximately 10 to 15 minutes until it cools, then add it to the dry ingredients. Place all the ingredients in the bread pan in the order recommended by the manufacturer. Program the machine for the white or wheat bread cycle, and bake the bread. When it has finished baking, remove the pan from the machine with potholders or oven mitts. Turn the bread upside down, and shake the loaf out of the pan. Place the bread on a wire rack to cool.

Z

Zucchini

From your garden, your grocery, or the garden of your neighbor, zucchini takes on a new dimension when it is baked as Zucchini Carrot Walnut Bread.

Zucchini Carrot Walnut Bread Recipe

---◆---

RECIPE FOR A ONE-POUND LOAF

1¼ cups wheat flour
1 cup bread flour
1 tablespoon dry milk
¾ teaspoon salt
2 tablespoons brown sugar
1 tablespoon butter
⅓ cup shredded zucchini
⅓ shredded carrot
¾ cup water
1½ teaspoons dry yeast
½ cup chopped walnuts

RECIPE FOR A ONE-AND-ONE-HALF-POUND LOAF

1¾ cups wheat flour
1⅜ cups bread flour
1½ tablespoons dry milk
1¼ teaspoons salt
3 tablespoons brown sugar
1½ tablespoons butter
½ cup shredded zucchini
½ cup shredded carrot
1⅛ cups water
2 teaspoons dry yeast
½ cup chopped walnuts

DIRECTIONS: Place all the ingredients except the walnuts in the bread pan in the order recommended

103

by the manufacturer. The zucchini and carrots should be added at the same time as the water. Program your bread machine for the white bread cycle, and bake the bread. Add the walnuts at the end of the first kneading or according to the manufacturer's recommendation on when to make additions. When the bread is done, remove the pan from the machine with potholders or oven mitts. Turn the bread pan upside down, and shake the loaf out of the pan. Place the bread on a wire rack to cool.

VI

◆

Problems, Causes, and Solutions (or What to Do When Your Bread Is Less than Fabulous)

The following list of problems, causes, and solutions reminds me of my gardening handbooks that list a gardening problem, then the causes and solutions. Just as it took a bit of trial and error to determine what was wrong when my flowers drooped— was it too much water, too little water, too much sun, or too little sun?—it will take some trial and error to troubleshoot the source of your bread problems. This list is a starting place and will help you narrow down the causes.

A Problem
B Cause
C Solution

Rising Problems

1. A. Bread does not rise.
   B. No yeast; old yeast; not enough yeast; too much salt; too much sugar.
   C. Check ingredients.
2. A. Dough rises, then collapses.
   B. Too much yeast; power outage; salt omitted; machine opened during rising.
   C. Check ingredients; open lid only during mixing stage; remove bread promptly.
3. A. Bread rises too high.
   B. Wrong recipe; too much yeast; too much light flour.
   C. Check ingredients, including ratio of wheat to bread flour; reduce yeast slightly.

Dough Problem

A. Bread is raw in the center.
B. Bread did not rise enough; did not bake long enough; too much liquid.
C. Make dough and finish manually; use another recipe; reduce liquid by one tablespoon next time.

Crust and Top Problems

1. A. Soggy crust or the top crust is shriveled.

B. Loaf left in pan too long after being baked; loaf placed in plastic bag before it has completely cooled.

C. Remove loaf promptly; when purchasing a machine, select one with a cool-down cycle; do not put loaf in plastic bag until it is completely cool.

2. A. Bread has a sunken top.

B. Dough too wet; bread not removed promptly from bread machine; bread rose too fast.

C. Reduce liquid by two tablespoons; remove bread promptly from the machine.

3. A. Bread has an uncooked top.

B. Wrong recipe used for machine; too much yeast, causing no circulation; recipe too large for machine.

C. Use correct size recipe for machine.

4. A. Bread has a dry top.

B. Inaccurate flour measurement; not enough liquid.

C. Check ingredients; add one tablespoon more liquid.

Other

A. There are white spots on the side of the bread.

B. Flour sticks to pan during mixing.

C. Immediately after mixing, check pan. If the flour sticks to the sides of the pan, remove with rubber spatula and mix into dough.

VII

◆

Bread Machine Dos

1. Use Fresh Ingredients

The use of fresh ingredients, including eggs, yeast, nuts, and fruits, cannot be emphasized too much. For wonderful results, be sure your ingredients are fresh.

2. Use the Timer

Your first few loaves will probably be baked on the wheat or white bread cycles. After you become comfortable with your machine, be sure to use the automatic timer. The result will be a higher-rising bread. The advantages are that you can wake up to the smell of freshly baked bread or come home from work to a loaf that is ready to be eaten. If there is any question about whether or not you will be home in time to remove the bread, set the bread completion time for an hour later than you actually plan to return home. When shopping one weekend day, I felt certain I would return home by 5:00 P.M., so, when I left in the morning, I set the timer for 5:00 P.M. precisely. One store led to another, and much to my surprise I looked at my watch at 3:45 P.M. and had to dash home from the large discount mall that was slightly more than an hour from my home. Just when I had discovered the perfect outfit, I had no time to try it on. Setting the timer for one hour later than I expected to return would have solved the problem.

3. Experiment

When you use the variations for prepackaged mixes suggested in Chapter IV, "Prepackaged Mixes (or Simplifying Breadmaking)," and then experiment with some of your own, you will be able to create an endless number of breads and varieties. It is even possible to experiment with basic ingredients as long as you are ready to accept a few failures. I varied the amount of salt from none to one teaspoon as called for in most recipes. In addition, I experimented by reducing the amount of fat in one recipe from none to one tablespoon. Imagine my shock when the results were really not that different from those obtained when using the amount of salt and fat called for in the original recipe. The top of the bread was slightly different, the bread may have dried out sooner if not eaten right away, and it rose slightly less. These subtle changes did not affect flavor, and the bread without salt and fat clearly would be welcomed by anyone on a salt- or fat-restricted diet.

4. Use a Good Bread Knife

The only knife that should not be used is a dull one. Remember, dull knives make cutting the bread difficult, are more dangerous to use, and often mash the bread.

5. Get to Know Your Machine

Machines vary not only in the size and shape of loaf they make or the features they include but also in their characteristics.

Some machines have buzzers that can be set for additions. Others make it easy to utilize a special whole wheat cycle that fosters better rising. Others make loud noises kneading or have noise from their fans near the end of the process. You can get to know your machine's noises and features as well as the recipes that work best in it. It is only after making several loaves of bread that you will begin to "know your machine."

Given the luxury of being able to test several

machines, I was able to see the variety of ways in which machines had their own quirks and how machines have features not often discussed in the manuals and articles. I learned that in my Panasonic I had to wait until after the first kneading to add fruit if I did not want the fruit to disintegrate. I also learned that a vegetable shortening on the bread pan made removal of the bread much easier, a tip that was especially helpful in the Hitachi, in which bread removal was slightly more difficult than in other machines. When the weather was warm and humid, less yeast was necessary in my Panasonic and Zojirushi.

If there are certain features that will be important to you, try to find out before you buy your bread machine which ones have those features. Before I bought my machines I asked my friends, salespeople, and just about anyone who would talk to me about them, why they liked their machines. I still ask.

For example, there is consensus that the machines with the heavier pan (Panasonic) makes a consistently dark, golden crust. If you want to make quick breads as well as delicious well-crusted bread, the Zojirushi presents a class act for a machine! Setting up the mixing blade in the Zojirushi takes a few more seconds, though. The Hitachi makes a delicious loaf, but I prefer to use it only when I need to make just the dough, not when a well-risen loaf is going to be shared with a friend or taken to a neighbor's house for dinner. This is because the bread from the Hitachi tastes fine, but the top is almost too symmetrical for my preference. If I didn't have the opportunity to test several machines, I would undoubtedly think that whatever machine I owned made great bread.

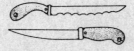

VIII

◆

Bread Machine Don'ts

1. Don't . . . Put Yeast Near Liquid Ingredients (Water) When Using the Timer

Because your bread may not start to mix for several hours when you are using the timer, you do not want the yeast to touch the liquid and start to actify before the mixing and baking processes begin. Here's a technique that always works for me: First place the liquid in your machine. Then add the dry ingredients, making a slight indentation in them and placing the dry yeast in the indentation. (Of course, if your machine has a separate yeast dispenser, this is not a problem.)

2. Don't . . . Use the Timer with Perishable Ingredients, Such as Eggs, Whole Milk, or Other Dairy Products

A timer postpones the combination of ingredients so you can easily organize *your* time *and* get a freshly made loaf of bread without distraction. But remember, dairy products can spoil if left unrefrigerated, so carefully consider recipes before planning to use the timer.

3. Don't . . . Forget to Clean Your Machine After Each Use

Even if you do not clean the machine immediately after you have removed the bread from it, rinse it out with warm soap and water before you place it back in the machine. When cleaning it, be sure to take out the blade and remove any bread residue from around the mixing blade or the mixing blade stem. Place a piece of paper towel or a sponge around the blade stem while you turn the bolt on the bottom of the machine. The bread residue comes off easily if it has been soaked in soapy water for a few minutes.

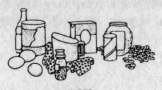

115

4. Don't . . . Put Ingredients for a Two-Pound Loaf in a One-Pound Loaf Machine

As ridiculous as this may sound, it is easy to make this mistake if you are using a bread mix. For example, whether the mix says it contains fourteen ounces or eighteen ounces is not always that obvious. Too much dough can result in a bread that not only hits the top of the lid, but may billow over the top, requiring an incredible amount of cleanup after the loaf is done.

5. Don't . . . Forget to Use Potholders at All Times When Removing the Bread Pan from the Machine

One of the key warnings that should appear on each bread machine is to remember always to use potholders when removing the bread pan. It is so easy to forget to do this, and the result can be a terrible burn. When a bread pan has a handle on it, you should never reach for it without potholders or oven mitts. It may sound obvious not to touch the handle or remove the pan from your bread machine without using mitts or potholders, yet in the exuberance of your retrieving the loaf from the oven it could happen. DO NOT FORGET.

6. Don't . . . Allow Children to Use the Machine Unsupervised

Because the bread machine is an electrical appliance and gets very hot, you must be careful about letting children use the machine unsupervised. There are too many potential dangers for children around these and any other electrical appliances. Children can watch and be part of the breadmaking process by adding in the ingredients, especially the peanut butter or chocolate chips, nuts or fruit; by pouring the water into the pan; or by helping form the pretzels. They should not use the machine by themselves.

7. Don't . . . Forget to Use Only Nonabrasive or Nonscouring Cleaners on the Bread Pan

Care should be taken not to scratch the nonstick surface. If you do scratch it, it is important to spray on a liquid shortening to keep the bread from sticking.

8. Don't . . . Remove Bread That Is Sticking to the Pan with a Knife

This can cause irreparable damage to the pan.

9. Don't . . . Open the Lid of the Bread Machine While the Bread Is Baking Other than During or Immediately After the First Kneading

Opening the lid will disturb the breadmaking process.

IX

◆

Hints and Suggestions

1. Use spray shortening for easy bread removal from the pan. A quick spray of shortening can keep bread from sticking to the mixing blade and pan. Although the pans are generally made with nonstick materials, the extra spray makes removal even easier and does not change the taste of the bread.

2. Lightly oil a cup or spoon before measuring honey, molasses, or syrup. This way the sweetener does not stick to the measuring utensil.

3. Make up prepackaged mixes. This saves a great deal of time. See Chapter IV, "Prepackaged Mixes (or Simplifying Breadmaking)."

4. UNPLUG YOUR MACHINE BEFORE YOU CLEAN IT. You can get into the baking part of the machine to remove crumbs by turning the

cooled machine upside down so the crumbs fall out. Depending on how many crumbs are left in the machine, you may want to clean the inside of the machine with vacuum cleaner attachments. You then can take a damp paper towel or napkin and remove any crumbs. Whichever method you use, be sure not to touch your machine's heat sensor. Do not use cleansers, steel wool pads, or abrasives.

5. Store your dough in the refrigerator before you bake it. Once you have prepared dough in the machine, you can store it in your refrigerator for a couple of days if you cover it with a damp cloth and every day punch it down to extrude unnecessary air bubbles from it. When you're ready to bake it, remove the dough from the refrigerator, let it come to room temperature, and proceed with the steps to roll out or shape it. You will use your traditional oven for baking your rolled-out and shaped creations.

6. To freeze baked bread, first let it cool completely. Then wrap it in foil or plastic wrap. Baked bread may also be stored for up to three days in the refrigerator.

7. Defrost baked frozen bread at room temperature or in the microwave, taken out of the foil or wrap, but with a paper napkin or towel over it. In the microwave, set the microwave oven on defrost, and follow the microwave manufacturer's instructions. Be sure not to overmicrowave; the result will be dried-out tough bread.

8. Heat unfrozen baked bread in foil at 350 degrees in the preheated oven for 10 to 15 minutes.

9. Cut your bread. It is easier if you first allow it to cool for at least 20 minutes. (This is very difficult when the bread is just finished and the kitchen is filled with the aroma of freshly baked bread!)

10. Store flour in an airtight container. In warm weather, store flour in the refrigerator or even in the freezer. The "pests" that appear out of nowhere in flour do so when it is not stored in a dry, airtight container. Even then these pests can appear. Various sources recommend keeping flour in the refrigerator or freezing it at all times of the year, although there is no definitive conclusion. If you are unfortunate and these pests appear, throw away the flour, and carefully clean and wash the surrounding area to destroy the next generation.

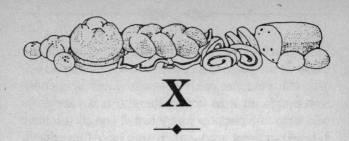

X

◆

The End, the Crust, the Heel

The end of this book, just like the end of a loaf of good bread, is the part that you can savor.

If the end is the first piece eaten (if you are the one who sneaks the end off the loaf when no one is around!), you receive a preview of what others will enjoy after you. If it is the last piece eaten, it helps you to think about the loaf that you have just enjoyed and to anticipate the next loaf. Bringing together the flavor and all the textures of the bread, the end has its soft center as well as its crispy, crunchy texture on the outside. It is also the treasured piece that is a great holder of jam, a piece of tomato, or sliced turkey or the perfect tool to dunk in stew or soup.

The end of this book should be just like the end of a loaf of great bread. You may have sneaked a look back here first, before you read the rest of the book. If so, you got a preview of the delicious recipes and creations you and others enjoy. If you followed this book in order, the end is a conclusion and time to reflect on how you will put all you have learned to great use. Either way, have fun, experiment, and use your bread machine to RISE to any occasion.

Recipes in This Book

INDEX

◆